(2nd edition)

Learn the "3 Easy Steps" to Marketing your next Garage Sale and what you'll discover is simply the easiest system to get more buyers to your sale than ever before.

By

Damon Nelson & Nicholas Bohn

Copyright ©2014 Dallas, TX by
Call Me Apps, LLC.

Table of Contents

Preface – Must Read Section 7

Introduction 13

Chapter 1 – Planning 17

    Goals? 18

    How Much? 19

    How Soon? 19

    When is the best time to have your sale? 20

    How should you organize your inventory? 24

Chapter 2 – Click it 31

    What is the one "Magic Word" you must use? 34

    How to create a Video from 6 pictures 37

    It may be ugly, but it works - Craigslist.org 39

    Let's use Facebook to actually make money 44

Chapter 3 – Stick it 49

    How to Make Signs that get attention? 49

    The History of the Stuckey Signs… 52

    The 10 best teaser keywords to put on signs 57

    Local Advertising that really does work 60

Chapter 4 – Sell It 63

    Inventory versus "Quality Inventory" 64

    How do you price your items? 64

    Leave some pricing room for bargaining 66

    Pricing guidelines. 66

Antiques & Collectibles – Are they worth any money? 68

Price Tag Stickers 71

Bundling 73

All items should be sold "As-Is, Where-Is" 77

The Big Day – "Day of Sale" Activities 77

What not to sell (or buy) 80

Chapter 5 – The Game Changer 83

Chapter 6 – The Seven Day Checklist 87

Appendix A – More "Tip of the Day" Listings 101

Appendix B – Room by Room Check Sheet 112

Appendix C – "Day of Sale" Layout Examples 121

Appendix D – Craigslist Ad writing tips 124

Appendix E – Garage Sale Classified Ad Samples 127

Appendix F – Recommended Teaser Keywords to use ... 130

Appendix G - Signage Posting Diagrams 133

Rural Destinations - Sign Layout 134

Suburban Destinations - Sign Layout 135

Urban Destinations - Sign Layout 136

Appendix H - "Supplies You'll Need" Checklist 137

Before the Sale 137

During the Sale 137

Appendix I - Recommended Cash Box Change 139

Appendix J – Complimentary Video Companion Course 141

Future Kindle Books by Call Me Apps, LLC. 143

Author Bios 145

Damon Nelson..145

  Nicholas Bohn 146

For Implementers – Bring Us to Speak at Your Next Event:
.... 147

Contact Information... 150

Prologue 151

Preface – Must Read Section

At Call Me Apps, we are always looking for new ideas that are innovative and geared toward personal success. When we first heard of the idea of Garage Sale Marketing, we immediately were interested to see if this worked. The idea of taking the traditional way of hosting and advertising a garage sale, and implementing today's internet marketing technologies made perfect sense to us. The fact is, that it could be taught in an "easy to follow" step by step system made it even more exciting for our team of information marketers.

When Nick Bohn brought this idea of using a few online marketing concepts and some very creative local advertising techniques to revolutionize how people found your Garage Sale, we were absolutely amazed at how he combined this together.

By doing just a little more than the average garage sale host, he easily doubled the traffic to his own sales. His results were astounding and almost too good to be true. His marketing efforts appeared to be fairly easy to duplicate. So we begin to actually test his ideas by having our own Garage Sales and helping family members host their own sales.

What we found was beyond just amazing. We found that not only were we bringing more people from our own neighborhood, but we were actually attracting people that were as far away as 50 miles from our houses. Not to mention, that most the people driving to our sales actually bought something instead of just looking. We took Nick's basic ideas of marketing online and creative signage, and then added our own set of time-tested advertising methods of lead tracking, online video advertising, pricing strategies, and day of sales techniques.

Preface – Must Read Section

What we ended up creating is a complete, easy to understand, step-by step, online video training course called Garage Sale Marketing, which can be found on our website http://GarageSaleMarketing.com

***

This book you are reading is the overall Garage Sale Marketing course, condensed down to the three main principals of the online video training course. We call it the "Click it", "Stick it" and "Sell it" method. Once you've learned these basic concepts, we then teach you how to implement these strategies in the final chapter. Specifically, we outline a simplified, 7 day marketing program, with a step by step daily plan for you to easily follow to host your very own incredibly successful garage sale.

In addition, we teach the "how to" and "why" on each of the steps of our "Click it", "Stick it" and "Sell it" program.

Preface – Must Read Section

Please feel free to add to it, but please don't skip any of these steps, because they all work together to bring in many buyers that normally would never visit your Garage Sale using traditional advertising methods. The more traffic means more money from sales.

***

If you are reading this book, then you're probably very interested in learning the secrets of making your garage sale both easier to host and a lot more successful than you've ever had in the past.

Let's face it, Garage Sales are actually a lot of work and oftentimes not even worth the effort, that's why you are probably reading this.

What we are about to show you are the same techniques that we use to market and host our own garage sales. The steps that we show you are easy to duplicate and are in a simple to

Preface – Must Read Section

accomplish; with very little marketing or sales knowledge.

So kick off your shoes, grab some iced tea and let's learn about GARAGE SALE MARKETING and how these simple marketing and sales tricks that we are about to show you, can actually make you more money than ever at your next Garage Sale.

***

Please be sure to visit the link at Appendix J – Complimentary Video Companion Course to get the free videos that go with each chapter of this book.

END OF CHAPTER

Introduction

For years there have been several good books written about garage sales, local advertising and "day of sale". For instance, Cathy Pedigo has written several books like the one she coauthored with Sonia Weiss called *The Pocket Idiot's Guide to Garage and Yard Sales* (Weiss, 2003) with some great planning and day of sale tips. And her other book *How to Have BIG MONEY Garage Sales* (Pedigo, 2002). In addition, John D. Schroeder's *Garage Sale Fever* (Schroeder, 2005) has some great ideas for "day of sale" and many tips on finding treasures at other garage sales that you can use to stock your own garage sale inventory. And finally the classic *Garage Sale Handbook* by Peggy Hitchcock (Hitchcock, 1986) is one of the very first books ever published that outlines a step by step guide to approaching a garage sale like a business that can make you money on weekends by teaching you how to host your own sales as well as getting paid to host other garage and estate sales.

And now it's time to add Garage Sale Marketing to that list.

WHY? Because of the Marketing, It's now a digital world we live, this method absolutely works, it's easy to duplicate, applies to all types of sales, and uses some of the best advertising and branding strategies ever invented. It's using magnetic marketing principals and attracting buyers from all around your area, just *like flies to honey!*

People are always looking for unique bargains. With the popularity of reality TV shows such as *American Pickers, Pawn Stars and Storage Wars*, it's not hard to attract people to a yard, garage or estate sale, especially if it's marketed right. In today's economy, everyone needs an edge. You don't need to be a Fortune 500 company to implement these winning marketing ideas for your yard or garage sale.

Introduction

Garage Sale Marketing is a new, refreshing way to look at an age old established event. Garage Sale Marketing has taken some of the very best online marketing and local advertising methods and shows how the average, everyday Joe (or Jo Anne) can market to the masses.

With the interest in garage sales growing all the time, it's good to see that there are plenty of resources to find marketing and sales strategies for having a garage sale. Our Facebook page at Garage Sale Marketing is full of great, easy to follow information. Garage Sale Marketing even has their own YOUTUBE channel that gives you information that you can't miss.

But, if you're really serious about making real money having your own sales and making money as a "Garage Sale Marketer" that changes people's lives and helps them with their own garage sales and eBay sales, then you've got to check out the complete course at http://GarageSaleMarketing.com

***

If you find this book helpful, please leave some positive comments at either Amazon.com or on Facebook.com/GarageSaleMarketing.

Thanks

Damon Nelson with Call Me Apps, LLC.

END OF CHAPTER

Chapter 1 – Planning

A successful garage sale starts with PLANNING!

Before we get into the meat of this book, going over the "Click it", "Stick it", and "Sell it" methods. We want to make sure that you have the basic idea of what you're hoping to accomplish with the garage sale, as well as have picked a good time and date for the "Day of Sale".

Proper planning is essential. "Never allow less than three weeks for preparation," said Peggy Hitchcock, author of *The Garage Sale Handbook* (Hitchcock, 1986). "It will take that long to decide on a date, gather and price your merchandise, arrange publicity, set up tables and attend to all the other details."

We agree with three (3) week preparation time to find the merchandise, price it, and organize the layout for the "Day of Sale". However, the actual marketing takes a lot less time than it used to, and we will show you how later in this book.

But first, answer these simple questions to get started. It helps to put things in prospective. If you can define your goals, it makes the vision of accomplishing them more realistic.

Goals?

Why are you having a garage sale?

- Clean out Garage/Spring Cleaning
- Making Space in the House: (e.g. New Baby's Nursery)
- Make Extra Money
- Get Rid of Former Spouse/Roommate/Family Members Stuff
- Want to Renovate/Refurnish
- Other

Chapter 1 – Planning

How Much?

How much money do you want to make?

Pick a Dollar Figure: $_____

How Soon?

When do you want to have your garage sale?

Pick a Date: _____

Just by answering these questions, I'm sure you feel a little more at ease. By answering them, you get a sense of resolve. You have just reinforced your original idea of having a garage sale. You are now on the way with specific goals in mind.

Chapter 1 – Planning

Now that you've figured out your goals, check with your local municipality, city, town or Home Owners Association to see what permits you may need.

***

When is the best time to have your sale?

When's the best time of year to have your garage sale? And a lot of people ask us and we've always said that just about any time of the year's a great time. However, what we found to be the best time is the springtime sale, an early summer sale or a good fall sale on a brisk Saturday morning. Each of these sales brings a different type of shopper for different items. Spring and Summer brings a lot of outdoor patio and yard equipment buyers. Fall brings a lot of clothes and toy shoppers.

Chapter 1 – Planning

As far as days of the month, we always recommend the first and the 15th weekend of each month, just after most people get paid.

Try not to schedule your garage sale on the same day as a major sporting event in your area or a major event in the town or city you live in. For instance, you would not want to have a garage sale on Sunday of Super Bowl weekend; now Saturday just before the Super Bowl maybe a good time to have your sale, while people still have money. You definitely don't want to have a garage sale on Christmas day or New Year's Day or July 4. The weekends ahead of those holidays would be a great opportunity to have a garage sale while people still have money.

And if you're planning on having multiple sales throughout the year at the same location, be sure the first sale of the year has the highest priced items because your first chance to display and show the item is the best chance at selling it at a slightly higher price. If

Chapter 1 – Planning

the same shoppers come back and recognize that item was here last time, they may think there is something wrong with it.

A few things to keep in mind during the summer time, the hotter it gets the more people need water. So always have an ice chest full of water priced at a dollar bottle. This will not only make you some extra money, it will give your shoppers a chance to cool off and a reason to stay longer. Another thing about the hot time of year, people will come in early and they will come in late. However, during the hottest part of the day from Noon to late afternoon, you have very little traffic. Whereas, the Spring and Fall traffic will be high early morning and midday; light traffic late in the day as it gets dark sooner.

***

Chapter 1 – Planning

Now let's look at what you are going to use for your inventory to reach your financial goal.

> **Tip of the Day:**
>
> Good "Rule of Thumb" for hitting your Financial Goal
>
> If your goal is one thousand dollars, you've got to have at least twice that amount in priced inventory to get close.

Use this simple checklist (Appendix B: Room by Room Checklist) to go from room to room in your home and start putting things on the list. A good rule of thumb is if you haven't used it or even picked it up in 6 months, sell it.

Chapter 1 – Planning

Walk your house, room by room with shopping bags or a few boxes to place items in that you plan on selling. Use the included checklist so you don't miss any potential merchandise. Merchandise = CASH!

Remember, this checklist is a guide, not a complete reference. If it isn't on here and you think it has value, PUT IT OUT!

Make an area available just for your inventory in your garage or your basement. As you place things in that area, assign a price to them. The more time you have to price each item, the better off you will be. We go into detail and discuss pricing strategies in the "Stick it" section of this book, as well as giving you our "secret ninja" trick for easily pricing an entire house of inventory.

How should you organize your inventory?

The more organized you can be with your inventory the easier it is for you to sell on the day of your garage sale.

Chapter 1 – Planning

Organize your inventory into like items. Keep your clothing, toys, tools, kitchen appliances separate so it's easier to lay out on your tables for display.

> **Tip of the Day:**
>
> # Clothes
>
> It is a proven fact that hanging clothes sell better. Just go into any store and see why. Use scented detergent and fabric softeners when washing the clothes.

It's always best to hang as many of your clothes as possible and wash and even iron if you have the time. Again the more professional that your inventory looks during a garage sale, the more you will sell.

Also, if you're going to have any items in the sale that need to be plugged-in, need batteries, or mechanical in any way; make sure that you can show the people that they work. Plug in everything that needs electricity and check it for yourself before the "Day of Sale". Make sure you have an extension cord and extra batteries on the day of the sale to prove that your items work and function in a normal manner.

Tip of the Day:

Testability

If you say it works, be able to show them! Make sure you have extra "fresh" batteries and extension cords.

Chapter 1 – Planning

Just because it doesn't work doesn't mean you still can't sell it. Put a reduced price on it AND mark that it "does not work". There are a lot of people out there who still like to buy items just to tinker with or fix themselves. A smart phone or iPhone with a cracked screen still has value.

Start diagramming the way you want the garage sale to look in your driveway and/or garage. When you get this diagram made it will be easier for you to start seeing how your inventory can be organized on tables and clothes racks. For a great layout example, check out (Appendix C – Layout Diagrams)

While you're still sorting your inventory and getting it ready for the sale, this is a good time to see if you have enough inventory to meet you financial goals that you set earlier in this chapter. If you're finding that you don't have enough "Quality Inventory" priced to meet your financial goals, then you have a couple options. You can either lower your financial goal or you can increase your inventory. A great way of doing that is by visiting other garage sales and buying their "Quality Inventory" and adding it to your own garage sale inventory.

Tips to getting the best stuff from other garage sales, is to be the first to show up and negotiate directly with the owner about bundling several of the more valuable items to get a better discount. We discuss "bundling" in the "Sell it" section of this book. Another method is to be the last at the sale and hand pick only the items that you think would sale and offer a very low price. However, if you wait till the end of a garage sale, most of the good resalable items may already be gone.

Make sure you can at least double your money when you're buying other garage sale items. Plus while you are at sales, take a good hard look at everything from their signage as you approach them, to how they lay out their

Chapter 1 – Planning

items. If they have good ideas, use them. You can also see what doesn't work.

And a final thought on increasing your inventory, simply start asking family and friends if they would like to contribute inventory for your garage sale.

At this point in the book, it should be noted, that junk that you would typically throw away, should stay in the trashcan and not be considered as "Quality Inventory". What we mean by "Quality Inventory" will be discussed in more detail in the pricing section of the "Stick it" chapter.

Working on your inventory and preparing it for sale is ongoing task up until the "Day of Sale", but in the next chapter we will start discussing the advertising and marketing your garage sale and why it is one of the most important things you can do to bring buyers to your doorstep.

END OF CHAPTER

Chapter 2 – Click it

"Click it" represents the Online Marketing method of our Garage Sale Marketing Course. Online marketing means advertising on the internet and is a fairly new advertising medium with constantly changing rules (aka. Google), social media strategies, video formats, SEO techniques, and advertising policies. However, the good news for you is that it can be very cheap to start (if not free), have incredible reach of local customers, be done quickly with immediate results, and the entire process can be repeatable using a few simple tricks that we have discovered.

Chapter 2 – Click it

> **Tip of the Day:**
>
> **Online Marketing**
>
> Reach more people with internet marketing. The web is WORLD wide!.

How can you tap into online marketing and why would you want to?

We can answer that with three words, VIDEO, Craigslist, and Facebook. Actually a Fourth is eBay for the more advanced users.

***

Video is the trick to converting viewers into buyers. Did you know that in 2013, over 90%

of internet traffic are video based AND that Visitors who view product videos are 85% more likely to buy than visitors who do not see a video on the web. (Specialists, 2012)

Now that video is so easy to capture with most cameras and smart phones, and that anyone can post a YouTube video with their phone's video camera or uploading from your camera; there is really no reason not to have a Video on your ad. It doesn't have to be great work of art, just needs to show the basic high dollar items that you are selling.

There is also a neat trick if you don't want to do a video. We discovered a free video creation website called Animoto.com. Where you can easily upload 6 pictures and have Animoto create a stunning animated video in Flash with music, then give you a link that you can simply copy into your ad.

Chapter 2 – Click it

What is the one "Magic Word" you must use?

So the "Magic" of our online marketing concept is very simple. Using the word "VIDEO" in the title of all your ads and placing a video link inside the ad.

Based on our link tracking test results, we found that ads with the word "Video" in the subject line of the craigslist ad in the Garage Sale section, gets 3 times more video views than ads we tested without "Video" in the title. How is that possible? We believe the stats stated earlier, that people want to see videos; and they especially want to see what you are selling at a garage sale before they actually invest the time to drive to the sale. In addition, "Day of Sale" informal surveys with buyers proved that most people that found the craigslist ad, actually watched the video before deciding to visit the sale.

Tip of the Day:

How to identify if your video actually works.

Place a picture of something of value "only" in the video with a special low price. For instance, only put the "40 inch LED TV" in the video, then when someone asks about the "40 inch LED TV" you know instantly how they found you. Advertisers have been doing this for many years with tracking codes and loss leaders.

People scanning ads in Craigslist seem to be attracted to titles with the word "Video" in the ad itself. And it makes it very easy to be noticed in a very crowded section of Craigslist. This doesn't cost you any extra and seems to work very well for driving traffic to our sales.

The other side of our simple online marketing strategy is using Craigslist.org. This is a free classified advertising source and is absolutely the best source for free garage sale ads to promote your own sale.

Combining the word "VIDEO" in the subject line of the craigslist ad, along with inserting a video link inside the ad, has proven to be the most effective form of driving online visitors searching for a garage sale in their area directly to your doorstep.

Let me repeat this… Using Craigslist.org along with "VIDEO" in the title line, and a link to the video in the classified ad is what we have found to be the MOST EFFECTIVE AND CHEAPEST WAY to advertise your garage sale online. PERIOD…

Chapter 2 – Click it

So let's get started on how to do this for virtually free.

How to create a Video from 6 pictures

You can use up to six pictures to create and absolutely wonderful video on a free program called ANIMOTO.COM. It's easy to use and like I said it adds a lot of value to your ad. Just jump on your computer and find ANIMOTO.COM on the internet.

Just follow their easy to follow instructions and with as little as 6 pictures, you can make a video and link it to your ad. You can add some text descriptions to list your street address, some of the keyword items, DATE and TIME of the sale and make sure one of those pictures includes one of your sign pictures. This helps the visitor identify your sale instead of other garage sales that are on the same day in your neighborhood.

There is a paid version that you can actually add a map link to the end of the video, but you don't need this to create a simple video. If you decide to get serious later on about making money with the Garage Sales Marketing course, then we would highly recommend the pro version that gives you a lot more options and allows more pictures; along with including a clickable link at the end of the video to take the visitors straight to your Google maps address. This version also allows you to download to YouTube or to any other video service as well as make a DVD.

The idea here is to show off some of your best inventory along with your signage and let the viewer's know what all you will be selling at your garage sale. Don't be afraid to put a car, boat or jet ski in the video. Remember this video is to attract attention and get traffic to your door. You may not sell the high end inventory, but it lets everyone know that your Garage Sale is more than just a junk swap meet.

Chapter 2 – Click it

It may be ugly, but it works - Craigslist.org

Let's talk about Craigslist.org. What I'm about to tell you will be the number one thing that will single handedly increase traffic to your garage. (Appendix D - Craigslist Ad Sample)

Craigslist.org is a great way for anyone to advertise a garage sale. So how do you stand out from the crowd? The way you do this is in the headline of your ad, use the word "Video". That's right, we recommend that you use a video to your craigslist ad.

Chapter 2 – Click it

To watch this video, just click the picture and log into your free membership account. If you have not signed up yet for your complimentary Video Companion membership, please see Appendix J – Complimentary Video Companion Course

***

To start with, a great ad is a simple ad, check out sample ads. (Appendix E – Print Ad Samples)

Second, let's give your garage sale a name. **THE MOTHER OF ALL GARAGE SALES, SALE OF THE YEAR, BIG TEX SALE, SEND MY GRANDMA TO THE CARRIBEAN** or something that shows this will be a big event and still has a personality. That name will be in your headline along with the word video.

Third, use keywords. Keywords are words that are important items that Buyers are shopping for at a Garage and/or Estate Sale.

Chapter 2 – Click it

You don't have to go into a long litany of individual items when writing your ad. Just list the major items people most look for in garage sales.

Here's a short list of keywords to use in your ad. For more keywords see Appendix F – Keywords

Tools, Toys, Electronics, TVs, Appliances, Furniture, Power Tools, Yard Equipment, Sporting Goods, Patio Furniture, Leather Recliners

Every garage sale has clothes. Unless you're being specific, like fur coats or a leather coat, clothes will not be a big draw in your ad. Just use those keywords to list what you have.

Fourth, put your address in the ad. I know it sounds simple, but it is very easy to forget. After spending the time to create the video and create the ad, it is all wasted if they don't know how to find you. Make sure you list your complete address and also any special

Chapter 2 – Click it

driving directions needed to find your sale on your craigslist ad. What we recommend is to add a Google maps link of your address into your ad, along with your written address and any special notes to find you.

Fifth, Add pictures of some of your best items to the Craigslist ad. You can even use the camera on your phone to take the pictures. Adding pictures make a special link on the search index to show that you have pictures of your items. Craislist.org has stated in the past that ads with picture icons in the search tend to get twice as many clicks versus ads that don't have pictures. The first picture should be of the shape, color and words of your signs. We will discuss this more in the "Stick it" section of this book. But for now, go ahead and create a sign and take a picture to include it as the first picture. Then add up to 5 more pictures to the ad.

Chapter 2 – Click it

> **Tip of the Day:**
>
> **Animoto**
>
> Six pictures are all you need to make a professional video with soundtrack!

And finally, be sure to list the TIME and DATE of the sale. We recommend not including your phone number. You want people to drive and find you, not call you…

Chapter 2 – Click it

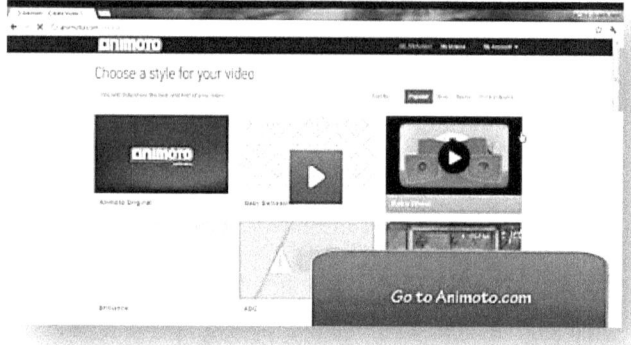

To watch this video, just click the picture and log into your free membership account. If you have not signed up yet for your complimentary Video Companion membership, please see Appendix J – Complimentary Video Companion Course

***

Let's use Facebook to actually make money

And here's how. While you're on the Internet go ahead and post the link to your Craigslist ad directly on your Facebook page as an

Chapter 2 – Click it

announcement on your wall, along with a short description. Make sure you let all your friends know you're having a sale, if you're active on Facebook this is a great way to get friends and family to visit your sale and all their friends too!

Now this may sound counterintuitive, in addition to the short description of your garage sale and the link to Craigslist.org, Go ahead and add a silly picture of a smiling baby, set of cute puppies, kitty cat or sexy woman to the post. You can copy these from flickr.com or Google Images. This picture technique is highly effective at setting this announcement post apart from all your other posts and get viewer's attention. Do this not only on your Facebook wall, but on other friend's wall posts that include your posts.

Then as an added measure, copy that post along with the picture and go out and search for the words "Garage Sale" and your city's name in the search bar and add that

Chapter 2 – Click it

announcement of your garage sale to their Facebook page if it's public. If it's not public, ask to be there friend and then ask if you can post on their wall.

And finally, ask all your family and friends to post a comment on your post and even make a post on their Facebook page if possible.

***

Chapter 2 – Click it

Lastly, I am including a few other websites that have a national listing service for garage sales. Be sure to read all their instructions and copy the craigslist ad description and title into these listings, including the video link and the word "Video" in the title

YardSaleTreasureMap.com at
http://yardsaletreasuremap.com/

Garage Sales Tracker at
http://www.garagesalestracker.com/

Garage Sale Finder at
http://garagesalefinder.com/

And for the items that don't sell, try listing them on eBay, Craigslist and Amazon. Remember, to make a new video with several pictures of that item and a good description of the item in the video, using Animoto. Like the Garage Sale itself, items online tend to sale better with a video of the item and a short description of what it is and the price.

Chapter 2 – Click it

If you are interested in learning a lot more about this online marketing strategy, we show you how to do this for both yourself and for others as a business in the online video training course at GarageSaleMarketing.com

END OF CHAPTER

Chapter 3 – Stick it

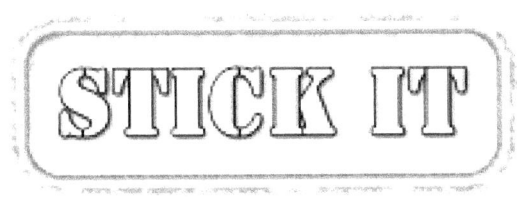

"Stick it" represents the local advertising method of our garage sale marketing course. Local advertising is all about placing signs in strategic areas around your neighborhood, space like a set of breadcrumbs leading to your treasure. Local advertising also includes placing ads in your local newspaper and on bulletin boards space in your community.

How to Make Signs that get attention?

Let's start talking about the signage you will need for your garage sale.

We strongly suggest you buy chloroplast signs with "H" frames that are of bright colors and

Chapter 3 – Stick it

unique shapes. *Lowe's, Home Depot* and most "do-it-yourself" stores have them.

We have had the best success using oval shaped, yellow corrugated signs and arrow shaped, yellow corrugated signs. They are uniquely different than all other signs. In addition, when you use them in combination with our "Stuckey Signs" method, makes it a very powerful message that draws customers to your doorstep, bypassing all other garage sales in the neighborhood. We have been told by several garage sale shoppers that it's like a scavenger hunt following the signs.

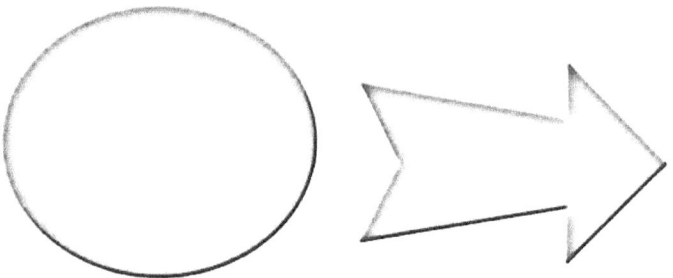

These signs are not the cheapest in the stores, but when these signs are used properly they

Chapter 3 – Stick it

more than pay for themselves with additional traffic and sales. You can use standard H-Frames with each and they can be found at most Home Depots.

This signage method has been around for many years, however it has not been used much in local garage sales. What most people are accustomed to is a single sign, or worse a cardboard box with "Garage Sale" printed on the side at the end of a street.

Let me first tell you a little story about where we came up with this ingenious method of creating and setting out our signs.

Chapter 3 – Stick it

The History of the Stuckey Signs…

In the early 1930's in Eastman, Georgia, Williamson S. Stuckey, Sr. had such a successful pecan harvest from his family's orchard that he offered a portion of his bounty for sale in a lean-to roadside shed. Florida-bound tourists traveling the two-lane Georgia 23 blacktop snapped up the flavorful pecans instantly, as gifts for friends and family and as succulent souvenirs of the agricultural south.

In 1937, a new building went up in which candy became king. The crowning glory in a profusion of nut-based confections was the now-famous Pecan Log Roll in a size for every appetite and every budget. Restaurant service was added, other fancy foods were stocked, and a souvenir section was installed to cover every whim from rubber snakes to sea-shell ashtrays. Gasoline pumps were a logical addition - all of it tied together with the signature teal blue roof. Stuckey's had come to

Chapter 3 – Stick it

life, and a new era of roadside travel service was born.

During their heyday, Stuckey's popped up along all the major interstate highways form north to south and from Florida to Arizona. They were very effective at attracting customers to their store by using a simple set of similar looking signs that had minimal wording, with enticing slogans, and were spaced about 1000 feet or more. They were placed so that driving down the highway, they almost looked like a moving picture show (at the time).

The Stuckey's logo was unique and stood out. All the signs had the same color and shape, so

Chapter 3 – Stick it

that you could quickly recognize the signs from a long ways away. Each sign had a simple phrase like "Ice Cold Drinks", "Pecan Treats", "Extra Clean Restrooms" or "Juicy Hamburgers". As you got closer to the Stuckeys' store, they started giving you mileage and turn directions, with the final signs ending in Next Exit or "You're almost there". So by the time you read all the signs, you were either very hungry or else very curious as to what else they had in the store to buy.

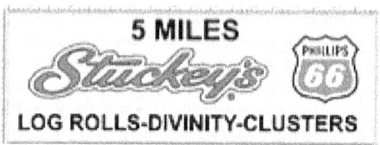

You may not be aware of it, but this classic signage and advertising method is still used today, very effectively. The best examples are casino billboards on the interstates.

Chapter 3 – Stick it

To watch this video, just click the picture and log into your free membership account. If you have not signed up yet for your complimentary Video Companion membership, please see Appendix J – Complimentary Video Companion Course

***

So how do we apply this little piece of history to our garage sale? Simple... We make our signs very unique and to the point by using the same color and same size sign for the entire series of signs, with short teaser keywords and directions to the garage sale.

In bold print, write on the sign the name of your garage sale, for instance "THE MOTHER OF ALL GARAGE SALES". In the center put just one word, such as "TOYS" then at the bottom put an arrow of which way to turn or how far to the sale.

Make sure your address is clear and legible along with the hours of the sale on the last few signs.

On each sign, use a different keyword for each sign.

Chapter 3 – Stick it

As people are following the route, they will see signs that tell the story of what is at the garage sale. How many do you use? We recommend at least 7 to 10 signs positioned at each turn off of the major highway or busiest intersection. NOTE: please check with the local authorities about any regulations regarding posting signs. We also, only recommend that you place the signs out early on the "Day of Sale". This signage method is incredibly powerful and you may actually have cars follow you back to your garage sale after placing these signs.

The 10 best teaser keywords to put on signs

Here are the teaser keywords that we use on our own sales and highly recommend you use them as well.

1. Toys – All Ages
2. TV's and Videos
3. Power Tools
4. Appliances
5. Furniture

6. Bedroom Sets
7. Electronics
8. Cars or Boats (if you have them)
9. Sporting Goods
10. Bicycles

This signage method is like leaving breadcrumbs to mark your trail, straight to your garage sale.

The closer they get to your garage sale; the frequency of signs should increase. People will start associating the color and shape of your signs to confirm they are on the right path. (Appendix G – Sign Posting Diagrams)

NOTE: After you're garage sale is over, go pick up the signs and save them. They can easily be reused on other sales, just be sure to leave the date off the signs when you make them.

Chapter 3 – Stick it

We have created a video to show you how to make the signs.

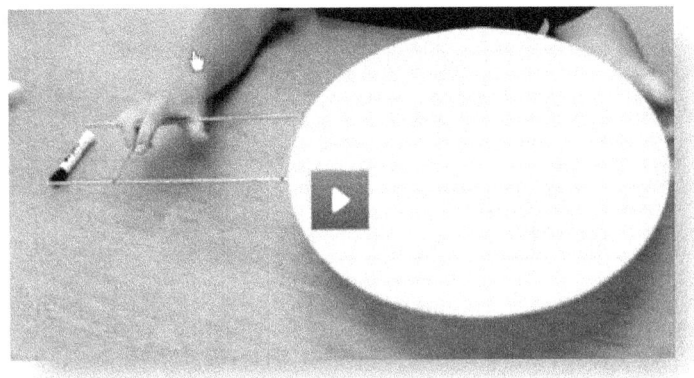

To watch this video, just click the picture and log into your free membership account. If you have not signed up yet for your complimentary Video Companion membership, please see Appendix J – Complimentary Video Companion Course

When you combine this signage method with your online marketing campaigns, this is absolutely the most successful and simplest method of getting traffic to your sale. We have tested on inner city sales, farm sales,

Chapter 3 – Stick it

urban sales and simple yard sales. It works every time!

Local Advertising that really does work

Some other local advertising that we recommend is posting an ad in your local newspaper. This does cost money, but a small town newspaper may give you a better chance at getting the non-computer shoppers. Run the same ad as you would on Craigslist you can even include the video link in the ad if you want. We do not recommend large newspaper ads, they are expensive and often don't get read in time for the sale. Stick to the cheaper small town newspapers and the weekly newspapers like Greensheet, Thrifty Nickel, and Weekly Ads.

And finally, community bulletin boards make for an easy and oftentimes "free" method for advertising your sale. Most churches, town halls, grocery stores, and cleaners have a

Chapter 3 – Stick it

community bulletin board that will allow you tack a 3x5 index card announcing your Garage Sale, be sure to include your address, date and time; as well as a few of those keywords. This may not be a lot of traffic, but it's usually free and gives you a chance to not only post the sale but talk to store owners and customers about your sale.

Now that you are about to generate a lot of traffic, let's talk about our final step in the Garage Sale Marketing course, the "Sell it" concept.

END OF CHAPTER

Chapter 4 – Sell It

"Sell it" represents the actual pricing and selling of your merchandise and is the third and final part of our Garage Sale Marketing Course. This is the module where we teach you the basics of pricing, how to do it quickly, and the best layout of your merchandise for selling and negotiating tips so that you can get the most money from your merchandise on the "Day of Sale".

Chapter 4 – Sell It

Inventory versus "Quality Inventory"

If it was trash when you originally stopped using something, chances are it is still trash. Junk, however can be someone else's treasure. "Quality Inventory" can cross a fine line. If an item has some perceived value, than sell it. If not, than throw it out. Old t-shirts may be hard to sell, but label them as garage rags and you may still sell them. But keep in mind… trash is still trash.

How do you price your items?

Once again, that's where shopping other garage sales will help. Get to know the market value for similar items at similar sales. Another great resource is eBay. Simply use eBay by looking up the items that you have and see if eBay has them listed.

Be sure not to confuse real value with sentimental value. Yes, the Styrofoam beer cooler may have been your grandmother's,

Chapter 4 – Sell It

but it is still just a Styrofoam beer cooler that can be purchased for five dollars in any gas station. Asking $20 for it would be unreasonable, but priced at $1 it could be an easy sale.

To watch this video, just click the picture and log into your free membership account. If you have not signed up yet for your complimentary Video Companion membership, please see Appendix J – Complimentary Video Companion Course

Chapter 4 – Sell It

Leave some pricing room for bargaining

Many people may not want to pay your asking price and will make an offer instead, usually on items priced five dollars and up. In order to compensate for this, you may want to add a few dollars to the item so that you have room to bargain. You can always come down in price, but it's next to impossible to get more than the stickered price. When in doubt, always price it higher rather than lower. A lot of people shopping at garage sales expect to negotiate and some even find that to be the fun part of garage sales. If you are open to offers and playing with them, then post a sign saying that "All reasonable offers may be considered". Then for fun, add another line that says "All unreasonable offers may get a "free no thanks" instead…

Pricing guidelines.

John Schroeder in his book *Garage Sale Fever* (Schroeder, 2005) has a quick pricing guide listed below, but he prefaces the list by saying "Check out other sales in your area so that your prices are competitive. Price according to condition and how new it is, about 10 to 25 percent of original cost. NOTE: Items should be clean; electronics should be working order."

- Paperbacks: $0.25 - $1
- Hardcovers: $1 -$3
- CDs: $1 -$6
- DVDs: $3-$8
- LPs: $0.50 - $1
- Videotapes: $2 - $5
- Color TV sets: $10-$25
- Black & white TV sets: $5
- VCRs: $5 - $15
- Clocks: $1 - $3
- Radios: $1 - $5
- CD player: $10- $15
- DVD player: $15 & up
- Lamps: $2 - $20

- Power tools: 25% of cost
- Single glasses: $0.25- 0.75
- Bicycles (older): $5- $15
- Microwave: $5-$10
- Games and puzzles: $1 or $2
- Children's clothing: $0.25 - $3
- Picture frames: $0.25 - $2
- Furniture: 20% of cost
- Power Tools: 50% of cost
- Pans: $1- $2
- Sweatshirts: $1 - $2
- Telephones: $2 - $10
- Framed art: $2 - $10
- Stuffed animals: $0.25 - $5

Antiques & Collectibles – Are they worth any money?

If an item is older than 1965, it may be a collectible. So, price it accordingly. However, just because something is old does not make it valuable. Research pays off here. Visit some antique stores in your area or a flea market and look for similar items on eBay and Craigslist. Ask a friend who is knowledgeable. If you are still unsure, ask for a customer's best offer.

By the way, a garage sale is not always the best way to sell antiques. A flea market, a classified newspaper ad or the Internet may be a better choice. You may need to pull from a larger audience pool to find that specific collector who wants your item.

What we recommend is visit some flea markets and price comparable items on "sold listings" on eBay. Don't use one of those online pricing services; you will have a better idea after visiting a few other garage sales and flea markets than the online services.

Inexpensive items sell best. We try to price items at 25 cents, 50 cents, and one dollar. If you have a lot of cheap items that are similar, consider putting in a box and post sign at $0.25 apiece. This saves time marking each item and can be used with "Bundling" pricing strategies discussed below. As prices increase, selling chances decrease.

Chapter 4 – Sell It

Price Tag Stickers

One of the items on this checklist is price tag stickers.

Price tag stickers will make your job a lot easier, not only on sale day but in your planning stages of the garage sale.

By putting a price tag on every item you have to sell, you will have a very good idea of what the full value of your inventory is.

Chapter 4 – Sell It

Just add the total of all the stickers together and you have the total if you were to sell everything.

> **Tip of the Day:**
>
> **Inventory/Merchandise**
>
> If you haven't used it in over a year, sell it.

We have included a simple checklist of things you need to start putting together to ensure a successful garage sale. (Appendix H – Supplies Checklist)

Chapter 4 – Sell It

Bundling

Also think about bundling. Bundling is the process of grouping things together to come up with a single price that is normally lower than all the items priced individually.

Why would you want to bundle? It's easy, to sell more stuff. There are times when you can bundle items you don't think would ever sale with items that will sale and get more for the item that would've sold alone.

A good example of this would be used CDs or DVDs. Say you have an old DVD player and you want to sell it for $15. Someone might offer you five dollars for the DVD player, instead why not offer to sell it at $15 but throw in three old DVDs for no charge. You just maintained the price of the DVD player and got rid of three really bad movies.

Another good example would be with old coffee mugs.

Price them at a dollar apiece or all six for five dollars. Your customer feels that they have saved some money and you just got rid of all the mugs.

Another great way to raise the price on some your items is to actually give them added value.

For example, instead of just selling the old crockpot, print up an old chicken soup recipe and include it with the sale.

Same thing with the blender, include a great margarita recipe.

The main thing is to not be afraid of being creative. Watch this video for some additional tips on increasing value.

Chapter 4 – Sell It

To watch this video, just click the picture and log into your free membership account. If you have not signed up yet for your complimentary Video Companion membership, please see Appendix J – Complimentary Video Companion Course

***

One of the best ideas I found was straight from Schroeder's book, *Garage Sale Fever* (Schroeder, 2005) in what he termed "Instant Ancestors". This is where I took some older picture frames and found some old prints of people, military themes and automobile pictures that he found on Flickr.com, then using Photoshop he converted to black and white prints and old style sepia prints and then printed them on nice paper with his inkjet printer. Then he cut them to fit into the frames and Voilà… He sales the framed prints in old frames for $10 to $50 apiece

Chapter 4 – Sell It

All items should be sold "As-Is, Where-Is"

Don't offer warranties, but if you say something works be able to show the customer that it does. If something is defective and can cause someone harm don't sell it in the first place.

People will always be looking for bargains, so give them bargains. Just be honest and fair with your prices and the people.

The Big Day – "Day of Sale" Activities

Let's talk about the day of your garage sale.

Here is a quick checklist of things you will need. (Appendix H – Supplies Checklist)

Make sure you have the proper denominations of change available. You don't want the first customer to buy something with a $20 bill and take all your change. Also keep in mind a local store that you can buy more change throughout the day if needed. (Appendix I – Cash Management)

If your garage sale starts at 7 o'clock in the morning make sure all your signs are posted and all your inventory is out at least 30 minutes beforehand that way you can check to make sure you have no last-minute loose ends.

Make sure you're not working the garage sale alone. Have your friends or associates work the sale with you for many reasons. One, to ensure your customers are being taken care of in a satisfactory way. Two, to ensure there is some safety in numbers.

Again make sure you have any needed extension cords or other things like batteries to test any merchandise that requires these items.

It might be a good idea to sell concessions during a garage sale. If it's a hot day selling bottles of ice cold water will keep your customers there longer and it's a great way to make a little extra money.

Never let unaccompanied people inside your house to use the bathroom. Let them know where the closest restaurant is down the street where a bathroom might be available.

Keep your tables organized throughout the event. Ensure your inventory stays looking like a department store's shelves.

Hold your prices for as long as you can. In the last few hours of the last day of the garage sale you have two options. You can either lower your prices or save the items you have left for your next garage sale or to add to a friend and family's next garage sale.

Remember, this book is just the start to learning this easy way to market and host a garage sale. After you've completed your first garage sale using these three concepts, you are ready to help others and make money doing it.

What not to sell (or buy)

Straight from the most recent issue of ShopSmart Magazine, a monthly magazine published by Consumer Reports. In their October 2012 issue, they noted on page 7 of the magazine a short list of what not to sell:

Cribs, car seats, and strollers. Items could be recalled or not up to the latest safety regulations. You are better off donating to a reputable charity that will check the recalls and safety of the items before they distribute them. Plus you get a tax deduction for the donation.

Food items or perishable. These are not legal to sale. You should only sell non-edible products.

Broken items. No one wants a fixer-upper.

Liquor. You'll need a liquor license to sell wine and spirits.

Mattresses. Bed bugs-need we say more?

Expensive items on the cheap. Do your research. That old painting might be worth a lot more (or less) than you think.

Chapter 4 – Sell It

END OF CHAPTER

Chapter 5 – The Game Changer

We saved the best tip for last, get this now and set it up. It is the Square Card Reader, where you can accept credit cards anywhere that you have a iPhone, iPad, or Android. They accept all major credit cards. No contract. No merchant account. No hidden fees. Just 2.75% per swipe and it sends receipts via email or SMS text messaging. Funds are automatically sent for direct deposit to your bank account.

 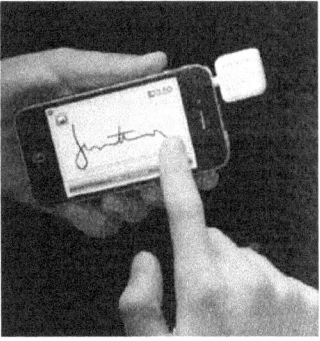

The cost of the reader is $9.95 and they can be purchased on Amazon or at your phone service provider. They even give you back the $10 as a credit to your bank account on your first swipe. So it's basically free!

No how do you use it. Plug it in and follow the onscreen prompts to setup. Now you can take credit cards at your Garage Sale, same as Wal-Mart. What does this mean for you…

There is no excuse why shoppers can't be buyers. If they don't have cash, you can still take their credit card and the sale is completed. No more holding items, while they go to an ATM machine. This translates into more sales and this makes you more money with a lot less hassles of holding items for those cash buyers that never return.

Now you can sell those high priced items and not worry about large amounts cash being in your pocket at the end of the day with hundreds of strangers walking through your garage. It also makes it easy to get the customer to commit to purchase if they don't

Chapter 5 – The Game Changer

have to pay for the items immediately, instead they pay their credit card merchant 30 days later or else pay it out over time.

***

GarageSaleMarketing.com offers the complete course available with videos, PDF's and step by step instructions on every aspect of garage sales plus a lot more tips and ideas of taking this training to the next level in earnings.

If you want more information, check them out at http://GarageSaleMarketing.com

Chapter 5 – The Game Changer

END OF CHAPTER

Chapter 6 – The Seven Day Checklist

This is the 7 day checklist that we use on our own garage sales. Print this page and post it some place conspicuous where you'll have to look at it regularly. It will help keep you on your game when planning and preparing your sale. Keep it with your Goals List.

According to our research, it takes approximately 3 weeks to have a planned, executed, and successful garage sale. We've condensed the steps to take into a 7 Day Checklist to keep you on task, even if you don't have a lot of time. *The more you can accomplish from this list ahead of time, the better.* Get started ASAP. Make changes if you need to. This isn't the only way to do it, it's just a list of everything you need to do. Procrastination is your enemy. The sooner you start the better.

Chapter 6 – The Seven Day Checklist

- **Day 1:**
    - When is your Garage Sale going to be? Pick a date: __
        - Try for the 1st and 15th weekend of the month
        - Avoid sale days that have a major sporting event or holiday (ie. Superbowl Sunday)
        - Also, fill out your Goals List so we know what we're trying to accomplish and when.
    - Do you need a permit?
        - Check with your HOA, City, and County to find out. If you need one, get one!
    - Where is your sale going to be held?
        - Choose a location. Keep in mind enough space to setup, accessibility, parking, and convenience. Chances are

your garage or front yard is your best bet.
- Let Your Neighbors know you're going to have a garage sale.
  - Do they want to participate?
  - Do they mind if you use some of their space if you need it?
  - Ask them to tell their friends and family to come see your sale.
- List your **Classified Ads** early.
  - Contact Classified Ad publications and set listings so that your ad will be in their paper on the day of your sale.
  - A week's notice may or may not be enough time depending on the publication. Try to do this as early as possible.
- Purchase Sign Materials

- Buy online at **Banditsigns.com** or go to your local home-improvement store to purchase the blank coroplast and H-frames.
  - What am I going to sell?
    - Start your **Room-By-Room Checklist** and begin collecting and organizing your merchandise in one location, preferably close to where your
    - Depending on how much merchandise you have, this could be a long process so break it up into parts. Start immediately.

- **Day 2:**
  - How many people will I need help from?
    - Draft your **Garage Sale Team**. Get commitments from friends, neighbors, and family that are going to participate and assist.
  - Visit other garage sales to see what works and what doesn't. Don't be afraid to use or improve on others ideas.
    - If you find something you think you can resell for more, add it to your inventory.
  - Post your ads for **bulletin boards**.
    - You can use 3"x5" Index Cards or cut regular copy paper to write them on or print them.
    - Post them as many places as possible. Review the list on the Bulletin Board page.

- What am I going to sell?
  - Continue collecting and organizing your merchandise, DO NOT GET BEHIND ON THIS PART!
  - Wash, Iron, and Hang your Clothing you intend to sell.
  - Take Pictures of your merchandise for your Craigslist Ad, Animoto Video, and Social Networking posts.

- **Day 3:**
    - Build your **Signs**.
        - Write in BOLD face and CAPITAL letters. Make your signs interesting and legible. Follow our sign making tutorial.
    - Make your **Animoto Video**.
        - Use our tutorials for the free and paid versions of Animoto. You'll need about 6 pictures. Share your video link on your social networking sites and upload to YouTube.
    - Post your Craigslist Ad.
        - Putting your ad up early lets people know ahead of time. You'll be refreshing it later so it stays on top of search results.
    - What am I going to sell?
        - You should have the majority of your

merchandise collected and sorted by now. If not, try to get it finished. This has to be done before tomorrow's steps.

- **Day 4:**
  - Gather necessary **Tables**, shelves, and clothing racks for displaying your merchandise.
    - Make sure you're tables are sturdy. Have tablecloths.
    - Remember, clothing needs to be HUNG!
  - Purchase and plan to sell concessions.
    - Packaged food, bottled water, and snacks. We recommend not selling sodas, since they have a tendency to get left open on tables and could easily be spilt on your sale items.
    - Gather tools needed to Play music and collect shopping bags to make it feel like a store.
  - Check the weather report for the day of your sale.

- - Prepare or reschedule accordingly.
  - What am I going to sell?
    - Price your merchandise using Price Sticker. Keep track of the sheets you use and the value of each sheet so you know what your inventory is worth. This should be a relatively quick process.

- **Day 5:**
  - Refresh your **Craigslist Ad** by deleting it, changing a few words and re-posting it. Stay visible by staying on top of the list.
  - Do you have the necessary supplies for **Testability**.
    - This includes extension cords, gasoline, keys, etc.
    - Make sure you have the appropriate paperwork and know the process for selling your Big Ticket Items.
  - Plan the **Layout** for your sale.
    - Where are the tables going to go? Do you have enough tables and clothing racks? Use our tutorial and guide for layouts.

- **Day 6:**
  - Check the weather report again.
    - Prepare or reschedule accordingly.
  - If you missed any of the steps, get it done now!
    - This is your last chance to make up for it.
  - If there is anything you can do the night before, rather than in the morning before the sale starts, get it done now.
  - Contact your Team and make sure they've still got you on the books for the big day.
  - Prepare for tomorrow.
    - Plan to get up early enough for tomorrow mornings tasks.
    - Get a good night's sleep!

- **Day 7:**
  - The Day of your Garage Sale is HERE! The BIG DAY! Are you ready?
  - Get up early.
    - Call your Team and make sure they're ready for the big day.
  - Refresh your Craigslist ad by deleting it, changing a few words and re-posting it.
    - Stay visible by staying on top of the list.
  - Repost on **Facebook, Twitter, and Google+**
    - Remind everyone your garage sale is TODAY!
  - Move your merchandise out of the garage and into the layout you planned.
    - Be flexible with changing it slightly if need be.
  - Set out your signs just before the start of the sale.

- You are likely to see you first shopper arriving just as your putting the last sign in the ground.
  - Open your garage sale and START SELLING!
  - Check out our **Day of Sale** module to make sure your day runs smoothly.

END OF CHAPTER

Appendix A – More "Tip of the Day" Listings

Keep in mind, with Garage Sale Marketing constantly growing, it would be nearly impossible for the list to be truly a comprehensive list. The majority of our tips make it onto this list, but the more time you spend in the program, the more you'll learn and the more tips you'll find!

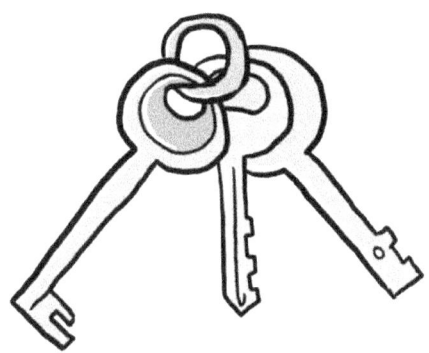

Planning

Proper planning will make all the difference. Plan the sale, then work the plan.

Appendix A – More "Tip of the Day" Listings

When

The best time to have your garage sale is when people have money. The 1st or the 15th of the month are the best times.

Where

Make sure you have the necessary space needed for your garage sale. Use your yard, porch or even your neighbor's yard (get permission first).

Goals

Goals are important. Write them down. The more visual you make your goals, the easier they are to achieve.

Reasons

The main reason is to make money!

Appendix A – More "Tip of the Day" Listings

Dollars

Pick a dollar figure! See if you have enough inventory to reach that goal. If not, you have 2 options - change the figure or increase inventory.

Supplies

Shop other sales to see what looks good and bad. Make a list. Use what works.

Online Marketing

Reach more people with internet marketing. The web is WORLD wide!

Craigslist VIDEO

Using a video in a Craigslist ad can bring your inventory to the people days before your sale. You don't have to be Spielberg or Lucas to make an effective video.

Animoto

6 pictures are all you need!

Ad Writing

Make you ad true. Make it easy to understand. Make it exciting.

Proof read it. Proof it again, then proof it a 3rd time before you post it.

Tracking

The more you know about your customers, the better.

Pictures

The camera on your phone is all you need for effective photos.

Social Marketing

Use the tools that are already easy to access, and easy to use.

Facebook

Posting on your "wall" and your friends "wall" will reach hundreds of people. Create an "EVENT"

Twitter

Post on your or your friend's twitter account. Reach people instantly.

YouTube

Your "Animoto" video could go viral. That's a good thing.

Google+

Let the most popular search engine work for you.

Appendix A – More "Tip of the Day" Listings

eBay

Use "Minimums" to make your "dollars" goal.

Local Google

Get your ads noticed 1st!

Link Tracking

Find out details of the people viewing your ads.

Local Marketing

Grass Roots marketing keep your neighborhood informed!

Signage

Make your signs stand out from the crowd.

Classified Ads

Print media is still a powerful tool for garage sales.

Newspapers

The bigger the ad size, the more attention it will draw.

Thrifty Nickel.

Make sure the price for your ad can fit in your budget.

American Eagle

The paper is free, but the ads do cost.

Bulletin Boards

Take advantage of public bulletin boards in your local area. They are read by more people than you think.

Affiliated Networks

Word of mouth is still the best form of marketing.

Selling Your Stuff

Don't throw thing away. SELL THEM!

Pricing

Don't let sentimental attachment sway your pricing

Inventory/Merchandise

If you haven't used it in over a year, sell it.

Room by Room

Open drawers, touch, move everything.

Shop other sales

Buy stuff if you think you can double what you paid for it!

Big Ticket Items

Ensure you have all needed paperwork when selling a vehicle

Layout/Display

A store like look will increase sales

Visibility

Put attention getting items near the street!

Tables

You can always sell the tables!

Hanging Clothes

Use scent detergent and fabric softeners when washing the clothes.

Organization

Create easy flow customer traffic isles

Day of Sale

If you followed your plan, Sale Day will be smoother.

Safety

You worked hard, protect your investment.

Cash Management

Start the day with adequate change

Sales People

Find the "entertainers" in your family and friends

Selling Concessions

Don't give your customers a reason to leave.

Testability

If you say it works, be able to show them!

END OF CHAPTER

Appendix B – Room by Room Check Sheet

Walk your house room by room with a brown paper shopping bag or a box to place items in. Use this checklist so you don't miss any potential merchandise. More Merchandise to Sale = MORE CASH!

- Kitchen
    - Loose Items in the cabinets and drawers
    - Small Appliances to be replaced
        - Toaster
        - Coffee Pot
        - Microwave
        - Can Opener
    - Dishes
    - Silverware

- Pots and Pans
- Cleaning Supplies

- Bathroom
    - Medicine Cabinet (no prescription drugs)
    - Under the Sink
    - Soaps, Toiletries, Perfumes
    - Brushes, Hair Supplies
    - Hair Dryer
    - Old Towels
    - Hamper/Laundry baskets
    - Toilet Tank Cover and Rug

- Master Bedroom
    - Every Drawer, closet, and cubby
    - Makeup
    - Perfume

- Jewelry
- Trinkets
- Shoes
- Clothes
- Hats, Gloves, Scarves, Belts
- Pillows, Blankets
- Baskets and containers
- Kid's Rooms
  - Include Children in getting rid of items
  - Children's Clothes
  - Baby Clothes and Items
  - Pajamas, Shoes, Socks, Underwear, Robes, Belts
  - Stuffed Animals, Dolls, Action Figures
  - Skates and Sporting Goods

- Games and Toys
- Old School Supplies
- Coloring Books and Workbooks
- Books and Movies
- Video Games
- Television and accessories
- Nightlights

- Linen Closet
  - GOLD MINE of FORGOTTEN ITEMS
  - Tablecloths
  - Sheets
  - Towels
  - Bedspreads
  - Cleaning Supplies

- - Board Games
- Living Room
  - Check every nook and cranny
  - End Tables
  - Coffee Table
  - Desks
  - Old Magazines
  - Records
  - Music, Movies, Books
  - Pictures or frames
  - Lamps
  - TV
  - Electronics
  - Stereo Equipment

- Computers and accessories
- Laptop you don't use anymore
- Furniture to sell and replace
- Office
  - Computer Equipment
  - Printers
  - Filing Cabinets
  - Desks
  - Furniture to sell and replace
  - Old Cell Phones and Accessories
  - Tablet PCs, Readers, iPads
  - Office appliances
    - Pencil Sharpener
    - Stapler, Hole Punchers, etc.

- Shelving
- Lamps
- White boards and chalk boards

- Basement, Crawl Space, Attic, Garage
  - Don't Be intimidated to tackle the hard areas
  - Furniture
  - Vases
  - Pictures
  - Appliances
  - Jars
  - Automotive Supplies
  - Hand Tools
  - Power Tools
  - Gardening equipment

- Sporting Goods
- Musical Instruments
- Lawnmower
- Weedwhacker
- Vacuum Cleaner
- Typewriter
- Posters
- Filing Cabinet
- Fireplace Tools
- Backpacks
- Hunting and Fishing Gear
- Snow Blower
- Space Heater

Write your own ideas for things you might want to sell but need to remember:

Remember, this checklist is a guide not a complete reference. If it isn't on here and you think it has value, PUT IT OUT!

END OF CHAPTER

Appendix C – "Day of Sale" Layout Examples

Take a look at the diagrams below, paying attention to placement around the edges of your garage, with clear pathways for walking an organized flow through your sale.

Proper organization helps with making your day smooth and prevents accidents.

Appendix C – "Day of Sale" Layout Examples

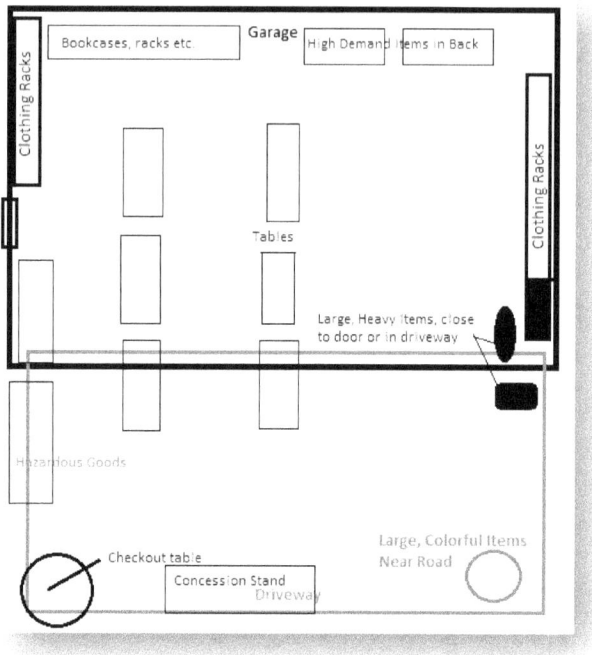

Figure 1 **GarageSaleMarketing.com** Original

Appendix C – "Day of Sale" Layout Examples

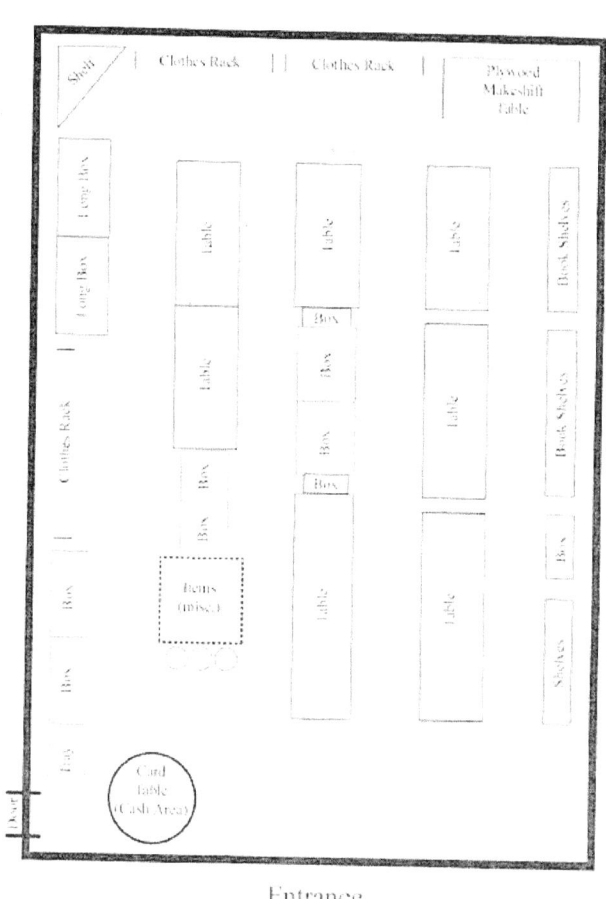

Figure 2 - How to Have Big Money Garage Sales by Cathy Pedigo

END OF CHAPTER

Appendix D – Craigslist Ad writing tips

Here are a few writing tips for craigslist ad or a newspaper classified from *How to Have Big Money Garage Sales*. (Pedigo, 2002)

Name specifically the major items that are going to be in your sale

Let the reader know that you have large quantities to sale, for instance loads of books, room full of toys, lots of unused paint cans, tons of tools, etc.

Give your garage sale a catchy name

Include your home address and the day of the sale

Make sure the times are listed when you're actually be up for instance 9 to 5 on Saturday

Be sure to include the video link in your craigslist ad

Appendix D – Craigslist Ad writing tips

Include a Google map link in your craigslist ad

Add six pictures to the Craigslist Ad. With the first picture being a copy of one of your signs, so people can recognize it when they looking for your house. The five other pictures need to be of the major items that you have in the sale

We always like to make ads stand out by making a very descriptive ad with many adjectives describing the items. Use some catchy descriptions of things that you have for sale, because ultimately what you're trying to do is make it worth the buyer's time to come and see your garage sale.

use CAPITAL LETTERS are **bold print** for emphasis. Be careful not to overdo it. Some people GET OFFENDED IF YOUR AD IS ALL CAPS OR THEY THINK YOU'RE YELLING AT THEM… See what I mean?

Appendix D – Craigslist Ad writing tips

Always enter ad with phrases like "loads more" or "lots of misc.". Always add "lots" or "tons" before your teaser keywords (assuming that you have more than a few). This lets people know that you didn't list a lot of stuff in the ad and that there is definitely more to see and buy when you to the sale. Try to create curiosity!

END OF CHAPTER

Appendix E – Garage Sale Classified Ad Samples

Poor Samples of Print Ads:

* Notice the authors use little more than their address and date.

* Several include their phone numbers!

* "Misc. outfits" is listed in one ad. Who cares about "misc. outfits?"

* We know they have clothing (I think that's what they are referring).

* "A little bit of everything?" COULD YOU BE MORE VAGUE?

Let's move on to some much better examples.

> **Send Grandma to the Caribbean Sale!!!** Garage Sale this Saturday and Sunday from 8AM-2PM. Furniture, Tools, Toys, TVs, Electronics, Collectibles. Even the Car is for Sale! Grandma is moving into a small apartment. EVERYTHING MUST GO! Come see us at 704 Howser Street, Bunkerville, NY

Appendix E – Garage Sale Classified Ad Samples

> **MOTHER OF ALL GARAGE SALES!!!** Tools! Toys! TVs! Even a Boat! LOW LOW PRICES! The more you buy, the more you save! Come check out our fantastic sale from 7am until 4pm this Saturday (9-18-12) @ **1234 Elmo Street in Dallas!**

Take a look at the ad samples above (yes all the addresses and phone numbers are made up). Notice how they use the name of the sale, complete addresses, times, date, and feature keywords. When you write your ads, whether it's on bulletin boards, in the paper, or wherever, keep this valuable information in mind.

END OF CHAPTER

Appendix F – Recommended Teaser Keywords to use

Use these keywords in your ads, signs and on videos as teaser texts of what you have to sale. For more information on the best ways to use these keywords, check out GarageSaleMarketing.com

- Tools
- Toys
- TVs
- Lawn Furniture
- Yard Equipment
- Lawn Mowers
- Sporting Goods
- Bicycles
- Furniture
- Recliners
- Dining Table
- Car
- Boat
- Motorcycle
- Jet-Ski
- Boat
- RV
- Antiques
- Collectibles
- Unique
- Rare

- Everything-Must-Go
- Moving Sale
- Rain or Shine
- Cleaning Out
- Multi-family
- Huge
- 1000's of Items
- Community Garage Sale
- Block Sale

END OF CHAPTER

Appendix G - Signage Posting Diagrams

Use the following examples to determine the best placement for your signage signs. We have numbered a path for Stuckey Signs (marked in RED) guiding shoppers from the intersection all the way to the sale. We also put X's (marked in **BLUE**) on other places you might also put signs.

The locations were chosen at random from Rural (Lehigh Acres, Florida), Suburban (St. Paul, Minnesota), and Urban (Dallas, TX) to give you a sample of each.

Appendix G - Signage Posting Diagrams

Rural Destinations - Sign Layout

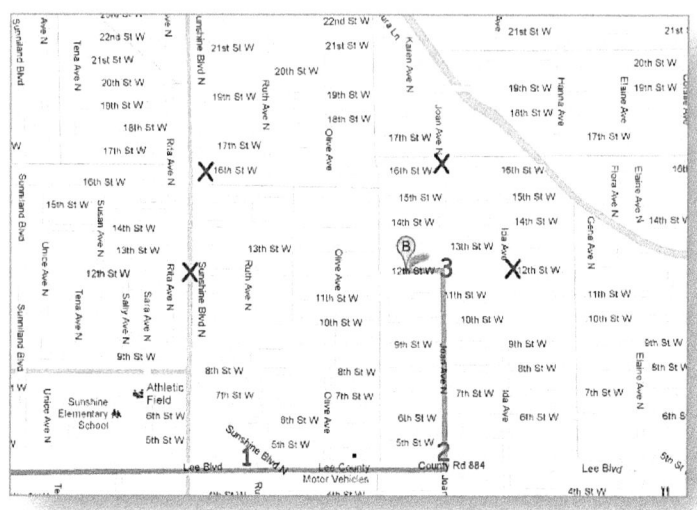

Garage Sale Marketing

Appendix G - Signage Posting Diagrams

Suburban Destinations - Sign Layout

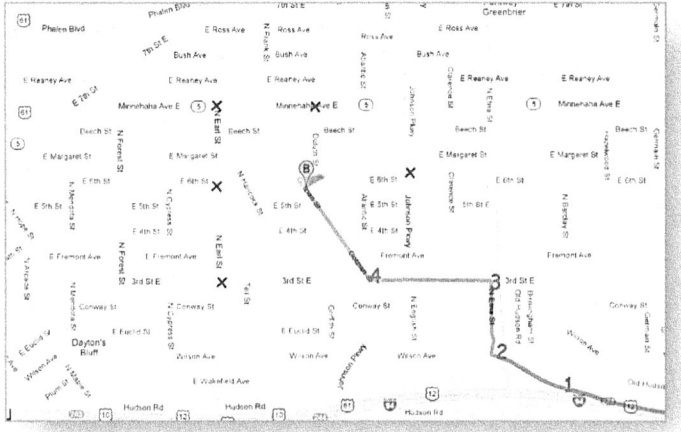

Garage Sale Marketing

Appendix G - Signage Posting Diagrams

Urban Destinations - Sign Layout

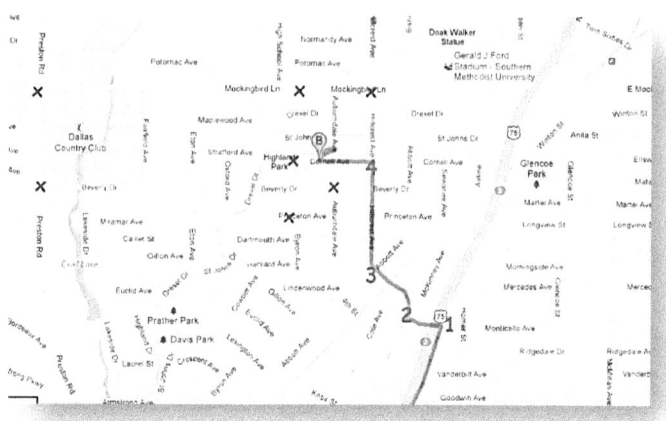

END OF CHAPTER

Appendix H - "Supplies You'll Need" Checklist

Before the Sale

- Signs (we recommend at least 6)
- H-frames
- Bulletin Board Ads to post
- Manpower to setup
- Price stickers
- Labels
- Balloons
- Cleaning Supplies
- Adequate space for sale
- Parking area

During the Sale

- Clothing Rack
- Hangers
- Tables
- Tablecloths

Appendix H - "Supplies You'll Need" Checklist

- Plywood
- Shelving
- Cashbox
- Proper Change
- Shopping Bags
- Newspaper/Tissue Paper (wrapping fragile items)
- Cooler
- Ice
- Umbrella/Shade for workers
- Extension Cords
- Fuel
- Light Bulbs
- Batteries
- Music Player/Boom-Box

END OF CHAPTER

Appendix I - Recommended Cash Box Change

Have the following change available at the start of the day.

Sales	Change Breakdown	Total
$200	20 Quarters 15 – $1 Bills	$40
$500	40 Quarters 25 – $1 Bills	$100
$1000	60 Quarters 45 – $1 Bills	$150
$2000	60 Quarters 60 – $1 Bills	$200
$5000 or more	60 Quarters 85 – $1 Bills	$300

END OF CHAPTER

Appendix J – Complimentary Video Companion Course

Follow this link to get your complimentary video companion course to enhance your understanding of the course materials.

http://garagesalemarketing.com/videocompanion

END OF CHAPTER

Bibliography

Hitchcock, P. (1986). *The Garage Sale Hanbook.* Lantana FL: Pilot.

Pedigo, C. (2002). *How to Have BIG MONEY Garage Sales - Third Edition.* Colorado Springs, CO: Winning Edge Publications.

Schroeder, J. D. (2005). *Garage Sale Fever.* Elk River, MN: DeForest Press.

Specialists, W. -D. (2012, February 19). *Web Video Statistics 2012 Infographic.* Retrieved September 25, 2012, from http://wecapture.co.uk/web-video-statistics-2012-infographic/

Weiss, S. (2003). The Pocket Idiot's Guide tp Garage and Yard Sales. Colorado Springs CO: Alpha.

Future Kindle Books by Call Me Apps, LLC.

1. **Just in Time Marketing**
   How the future of mobile marketing is going to change the way that we shop, and how we buy. It is a matter of fact that our smart phones are a way of life. How would you like to think about a product or service and instantly get a coupon and reviews of the services delivered effortlessly to your phone, with a friendly shopping advisor showing you other purchase options before you buy.

2. **Online Marketing Blueprint**
   Rules and Guidelines Every Business Must Learn for Mobile, Online, Video Webinars, and Social Media Marketing.

3. **Making Money with Meetup**
   Turning Social Meetings into friends, networking and money

4. **The Basics: Bartending Guide**
   Necessities for stocking your home bar and making some of the most famous drinks in the world. This simple guide will ensure you

can easily entertain with a fully stocked bar in your home. With these tips, you will be able to satisfy most of your guest's wishes for any home entertaining event.

5. **So You Want to Own a Restaurant**
Myths and Mistakes of investing in a restaurant. The top 10 reasons most restaurants fail and how to avoid them. A successful restaurant takes more than just a few good recipes and knowing how to cook.

6. **The Urban Tribe**
The importance of a surrogate family in today's world. Family support is essential in every one's life, but in today's transient world, people look for substitute families to cope with the ups and down in everyday living. The Urban Tribe is more prevalent then you think.

END OF CHAPTER

Author Bios

Damon Nelson

Damon Nelson is founder of Call Me Apps, the premier mobile marketing agency in Dallas, TX. Specializing in getting businesses new clients and actively engaging existing clients with automated 24/7 SMS lead generation systems. Mr. Nelson has over 20 years of experience in marketing both online and with traditional print media for many business types.

Author Bios

Nicholas Bohn

Nicholas Bohn is a successful marketer and public speaker specializing in training others to use skills from their everyday jobs in new ways to improve their quality of life. Through the GarageSaleMarketing.com system, Nick teaches how applying marketing concepts from the web, print media, and traditional advertising joined together with common sense and proper planning can help turn an ordinary garage or yard sale into a cash cow that is fun to do!

END OF CHAPTER

For Implementers – Bring Us to Speak at Your Next Event:

Want us to speak at your next event?

Call Me Apps, LLC is a full service online marketing agency. Our programs are designed to optimize any local business online marketing strategies that require new customer leads on a daily basis. Our agency focuses on advanced SEO (Search Engine Optimization) and Local Search as an alternative means to traditional marketing.

Our two managing partners who perform this educational session have years of speaking experience in presenting, educating and entertaining audiences.

For Implementers – Bring Us to Speak at Your Next Event:

Our Programs:

We offer several different programs including:

1) Websites, Google, and More: Getting Clients Online the Ethics, Pitfalls, and Techniques

2) Turning Clicks into Clients: The Ultimate Presentation for Online Marketing. This is our most popular speaking topic.

3) Social Media and Your Company: How to Leverage and Convert Clicks Into New Clients With Facebook, Twitter, Linkedin, and Google+

4) Reputation Management: How to teach your kids about how to manage their online presence to avoid cyber-bullies, protect their identity, and preserve their character for future employer searches.

For Implementers – Bring Us to Speak at Your Next Event:

This list changes from time-to-time depending on technology and demand. For a complete list of topics please contact us at admin@callmeapps.com

Inquire How You Can Book Us To Speak For FREE!

Every year our publisher subsidizes us to speak to a limited number of groups and associations at no cost to them. To inquire about having us speak at your event for no additional charge contact us at: **Damon@CallMeApps.com**

END OF CHAPTER

Contact Information

Phone: (214) 965-0852

Email: Damon@CallMeApps.com

Web: http://CallMeApps.com

For more Great Ideas and Step-by-Step Video Tutorials, please check out GarageSaleMarketing.com

END OF CHAPTER

Prologue

Thank you for reading this book. If you would like additional information, please check out the full video training course on our website http://GarageSaleMarketing.com

Or contact the publisher at CallMeApps.com

www.ingramcontent.com/pod-product-compliance
Lightning Source LLC
Chambersburg PA
CBHW051707170526
45167CB00002B/574